STARTER
Imagine
WORKBOOK

Gregg Schroeder

COURSE CONSULTANTS

Elaine Boyd

Paul Dummett

**NATIONAL
GEOGRAPHIC
LEARNING**

Australia • Brazil • Canada • Mexico • Singapore • United Kingdom • United States

National Geographic Learning,
a Cengage Company

***Imagine* Starter Workbook**

Author: Gregg Schroeder

Course Consultants: Elaine Boyd, Paul Dummett

Publisher: Rachael Gibbon

Executive Editor: Joanna Freer

Project Manager: Samantha Grey

Editorial Assistant: Polly McLachlan

Director of Global Marketing: Ian Martin

Product Marketing Manager: Fernanda De Oliveira

Heads of Strategic Marketing:

  Charlotte Ellis (Europe, Middle East and Africa)

  Justin Kaley (Asia and Greater China)

  Irina Pereyra (Latin America)

Senior Content Project Manager: Beth McNally

Senior Media Researcher: Leila Hishmeh

Senior Art Director: Brenda Carmichael

Operations Support: Rebecca G. Barbush, Hayley
  Chwazik-Gee

Manufacturing Manager: Eyvett Davis

Composition: Composure

For permission to use material from this text or product, submit all requests online at **cengage.com/permissions**
Further permissions questions can be emailed to **permissionrequest@cengage.com**

ISBN: 978-0-357-91181-5

National Geographic Learning
Cheriton House, North Way,
Andover, Hampshire, SP10 5BE
United Kingdom

Locate your local office at **international.cengage.com/region**

Visit National Geographic Learning online at **ELTNGL.com**
Visit our corporate website at **www.cengage.com**

Printed in the United Kingdom by Ashford Colour Press
Print Number: 01 Print Year: 2022

STARTER
Imagine WORKBOOK

A **Listen and circle.** 🎧 TR: 0.1

1.

2.

B **Colour** *Hello.*

C Draw a picture of you.

Lesson 1 Vocabulary

A **Listen.** Write a tick (✓) or a cross (✗). 🎧 TR: 1.1

1. ✓

2.

3.

4.

5.

6.

B **Point and say.**

1.

2.

3.

A Listen and circle. TR: 1.2

1.
2.
3.

B Match and say.

1.

a.

2.

b.

3.

c.

A Listen and circle. 🎧 TR: 1.3

1.

3.

2.

B Listen and tick (✓). 🎧 TR: 1.4

1.
 My name's Yara. ☐  My name's Kai. ☐

2.
 My name's Yara. ☐  My name's Kai. ☐

A Trace and write.

Aa
apple

Bb
bag

Cc
cake

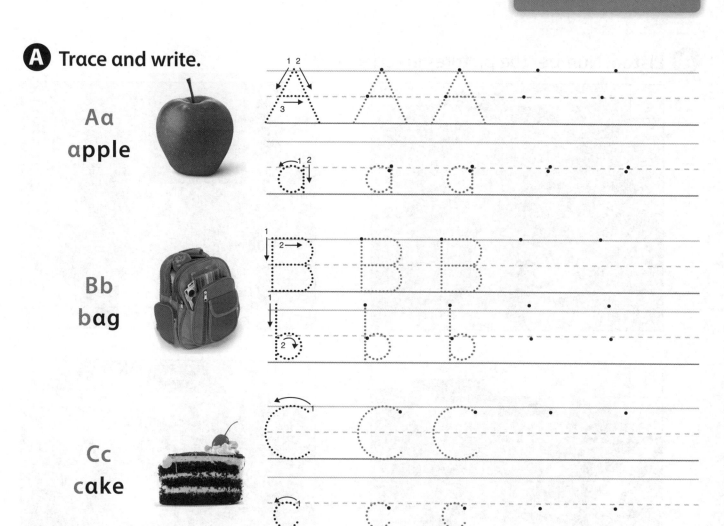

B Colour the letters *Aa*, *Bb* and *Cc*.

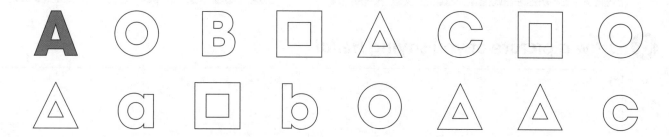

C Listen. Circle the first letter. 🎧TR: 1.5

1. a   b   ⓒ
2. a   b   c
3. a   b   c
4. a   b   c
5. a   b   c
6. a   b   c

A **Listen.** Number the pictures in order. 🎧 TR: 1.6

B **Draw a picture of you saying** *Hello!*

VALUE

Be friendly.

A Look and tick (✓).

1.

2.

3.

B Draw.

Be friendly.

2 At School

Lesson 1 Vocabulary

A Listen and circle. TR: 2.1

1.

2.

3.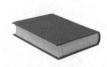

4.

5.

6.

B What's next? Circle and say.

1.

2.

3.

12

A **Listen.** Write a tick (✓) or a cross (✗). 🎧 TR: 2.2

1. ☐   2. ☐   3. ☐   4. ☐   5. ☐

B **Colour.** Listen, point and say. 🎧 TR: 2.3

It's a pencil.

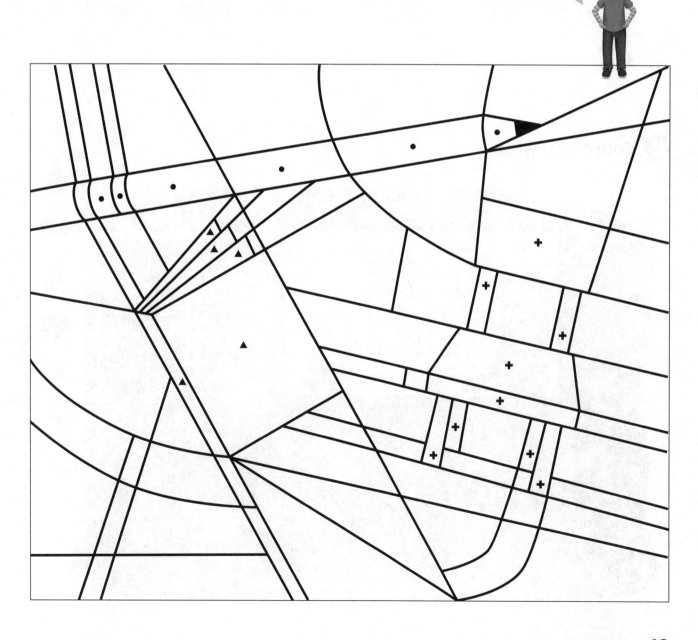

A Listen and colour. 🎧 TR: 2.4

1.

2.

3.

4.

B Count and write.

A Trace and write.

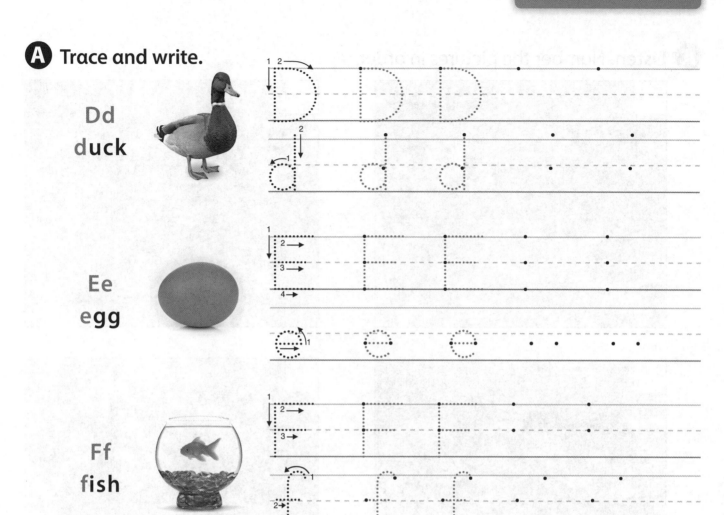

Dd
d**uck**

Ee
e**gg**

Ff
f**ish**

B Colour the letters *Dd*, *Ee* and *Ff*.

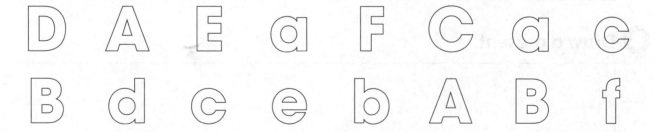

C Listen. Circle the first letter. TR: 2.5

1. d   e   f
2. d   e   f
3. d   e   f
4. d   e   f
5. d   e   f
6. d   e   f

A **Listen.** Number the pictures in order. 🎧TR: 2.6

B Draw a present.

VALUE

Say thank you.

A Look and tick (✓).

1.

2.

3.

B Draw.

Say thank you.

A **Listen.** Write a tick (✓) or a cross (✗). 🎧 TR: 2.7

1. ☐ 2. ☐ 3. ☐ 4. ☐ 5. ☐ 6. ☐

B **Match and say.**

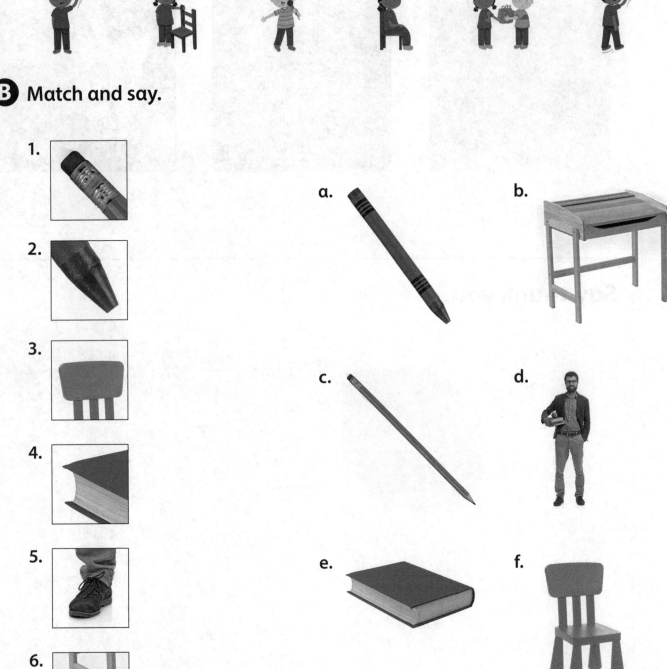

1.

2.

3.

4.

5.

6.

a.

b.

c.

d.

e.

f.

C **Listen.** Write the number. 🎧 TR: 2.8

1

D Draw and say the numbers.

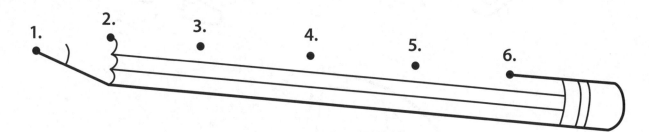

3 Toys

A **Listen.** Write a tick (✓) or a cross (✗). 🎧 TR: 3.1

1. ☐ 2. ☐ 3. ☐ 4. ☐ 5. ☐ 6. ☐

B **Trace and say.** Colour your favourite.

20

A **Listen.** Write the number. 🎧 TR: 3.2

B **What's this?** Point and say.

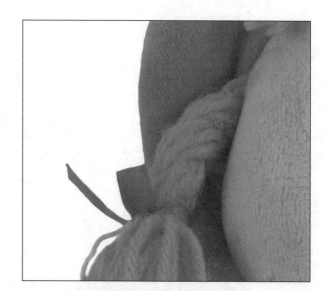

A Listen and colour. 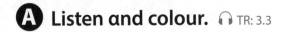 TR: 3.3

1.   2.   3.   4.

5. 6.   7.   8.

B Colour. Use Activity A. Then listen, point and say. TR: 3.4

It's yellow.

A Trace and write.

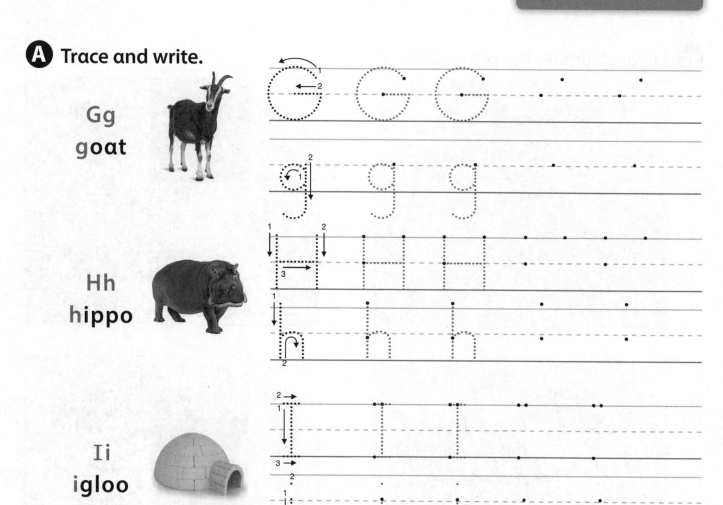

Gg
goat

Hh
hippo

Ii
igloo

B Colour the letters *Gg*, *Hh* and *Ii*.

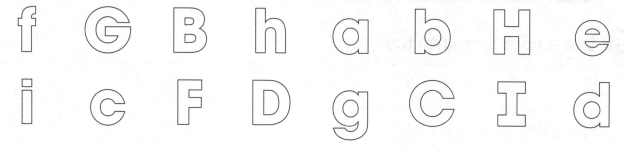

C Listen. Circle the first letter. 🎧 TR: 3.5

1. g   h   i   **2.** g   h   i   **3.** g   h   i

4. g   h   i   **5.** g   h   i   **6.** g   h   i

A **Listen.** Number the pictures in order. 🎧 TR: 3.6

B **Draw your favourite toy.**

VALUE

Be careful.

A Look and tick (✓).

1.

2.

3.

B Draw.

Be careful.

4 Farm Animals

A Listen and circle. 🎧 TR: 4.1

1.
2.
3.

4.
5.
6.

B Match and say.

1.

a.

b.

2.

3.

c.

4.

d.

5.

e.

A **Listen.** Write a tick (✓) or a cross (✗). 🎧 TR: 4.2

1.

2.

3.

4.

5.

6.

B **What are they?** Point and say.

1.

3.

2.

4.

A **Listen and count.** Write the number. 🎧 TR: 4.3

B **Count and say.** Write the number.

1. [6] + [3] = [9]

2. ☐ + ☐ = ☐

3. ☐ + ☐ = ☐

4. ☐ + ☐ = ☐

A **Trace and write.**

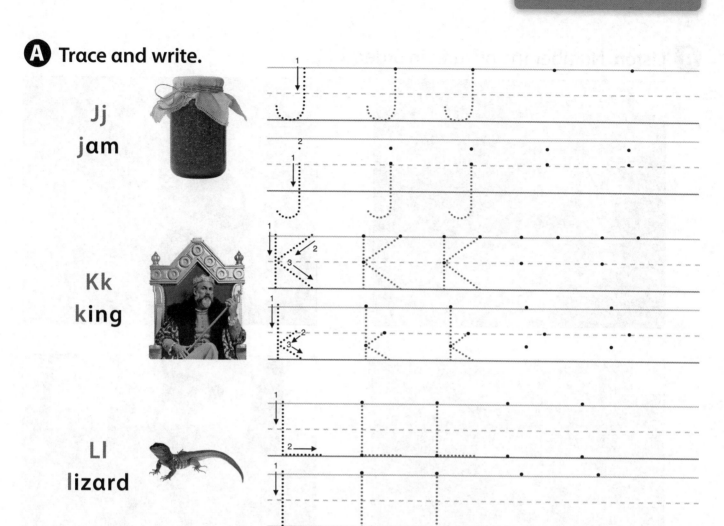

Jj
jam

Kk
king

Ll
lizard

B **Colour the letters** *Jj*, *Kk* **and** *Ll*.

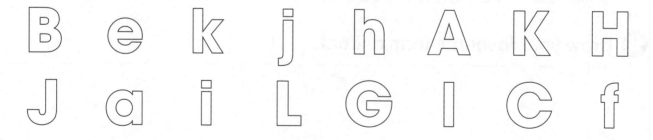

C **Listen.** Circle the first letter. TR: 4.4

1. j   k   l   2. j   k   l   3. j   k   l

4. j   k   l   5. j   k   l   6. j   k   l

A **Listen.** Number the pictures in order. TR: 4.5

B Draw your favourite farm animal.

VALUE

Make friends.

A Look and tick (✓).

1.

2.

3.

B Draw.

Make friends.

A Listen, colour and say. 🎧 TR: 4.6

1.

2.

3.

4.

B **What's different?** Listen, point and say. 🎧 TR: 4.7

Two big horses.

Two small horses.

C **Colour.** Point and say.

D **Match and count.** Then listen, point and say. 🎧 TR: 4.8

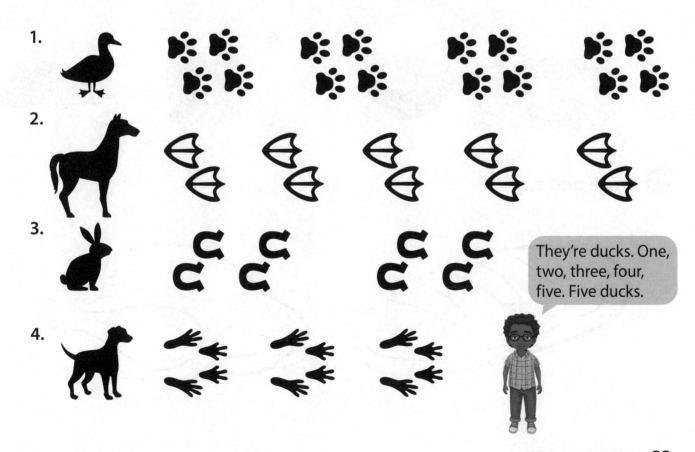

They're ducks. One, two, three, four, five. Five ducks.

5 I Like Food!

Lesson 1 Vocabulary

A Listen and circle. 🎧 TR: 5.1

1.

4.

2.

5.

3.

6.

B Trace and say.

1.

2.

A **Listen and point.** Put what he likes on the table. 🎧 TR: 5.2

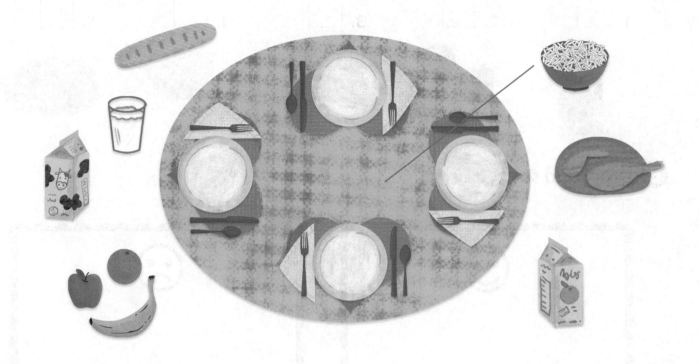

B **Colour and say.** 🎧 TR: 5.3

I like chicken.

A **Listen.** Write a tick (✓) for *like* or a cross (✗) for *don't like.* 🎧 TR: 5.4

1. ☐

2. ☐

3. ☐

4. ☐

5. ☐

B **Draw and say.** 🎧 TR: 5.5

I like juice. I don't like chicken.

A Trace and write.

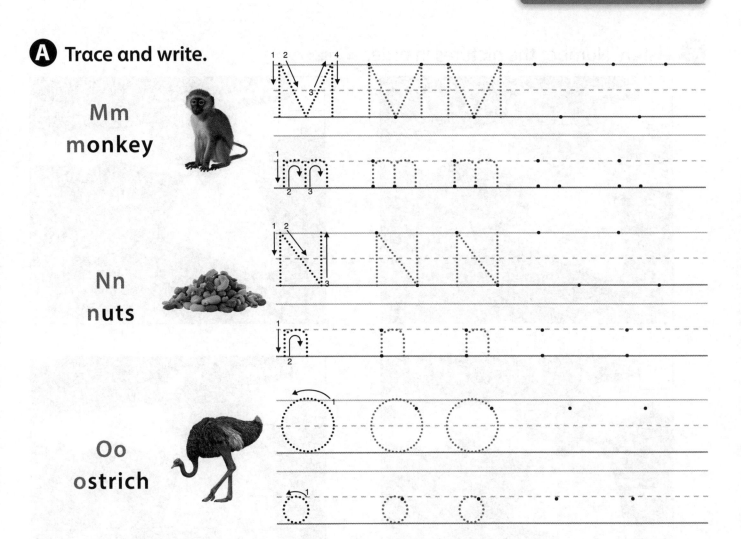

Mm
monkey

Nn
nuts

Oo
ostrich

B Colour the letters *Mm, Nn* and *Oo.*

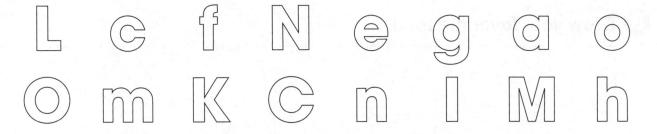

L c f N e g a o
O m K C n l M h

C Listen. Circle the first letter. TR: 5.6

1. m n o   2. m n o   3. m n o

4. m n o   5. m n o   6. m n o

A **Listen.** Number the pictures in order. ○ TR: 5.7

B **Draw your favourite food.**

VALUE

Give and share.

A Look and tick (✓).

1.

2.

3.

B Draw.

Give and share.

6 How Are You?

A Match the opposites.

1.

2.

3.

a.

b.

c.

B Point and say.

1.

2.

3.

4.

5.

6.

40

A **Listen and match.** 🎧 TR: 6.1

B **How are you?** Point and say.

1.

2.

3.

4.

5.

6.

A **Listen and match.** 🎧 TR: 6.2

1.

2.

3.

4.

a.

b.

c.

d.

B **Circle and say.** 🎧 TR: 6.3

I want chicken.

A Trace and write.

Pp
pencil

Qq
quilt

Rr
rain

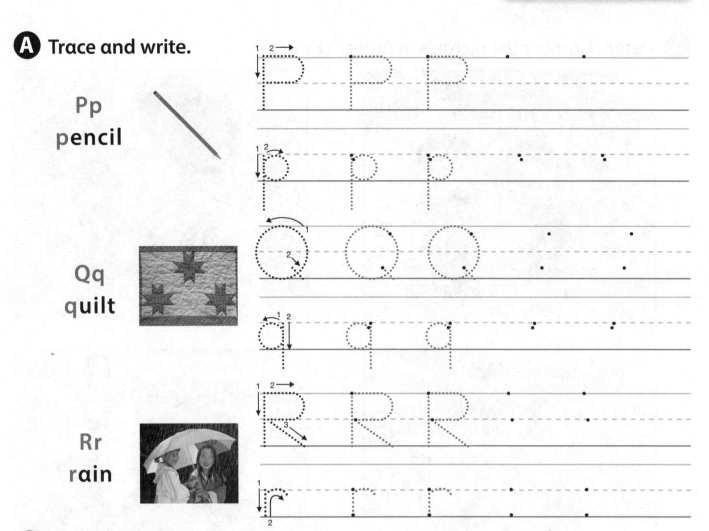

B Colour the letters *Pp*, *Qq* and *Rr*.

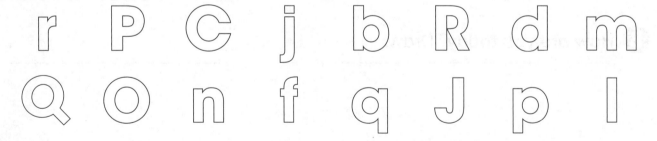

C Listen. Circle the first letter. 🎧 TR: 6.4

1. p   q   r   2. p   q   r   3. p   q   r

4. p   q   r   5. p   q   r   6. p   q   r

A **Listen.** Number the pictures in order. 🎧 TR: 6.5

B **How are you today?** Draw.

VALUE

Make good choices.

A Look and tick (✓).

1.

2.

3.

B Draw.

Make good choices.

A Listen and number. 🎧 TR: 6.6

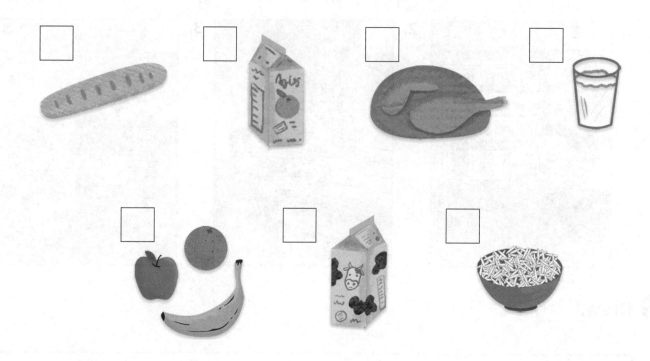

B Listen and circle. 🎧 TR: 6.7

1.

2.

3.

4.

5.

6.

C Write a tick (✓) for *like* or a cross (✗) for *don't like*. Then say.

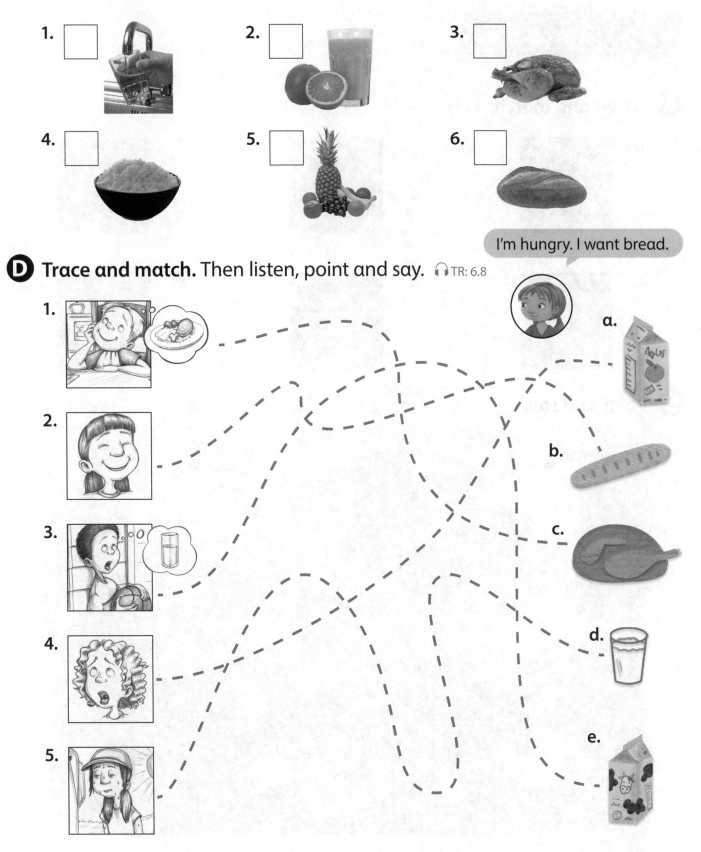

1.

2.

3.

4.

5.

6.

I'm hungry. I want bread.

D Trace and match. Then listen, point and say. 🎧 TR: 6.8

1.

2.

3.

4.

5.

a.

b.

c.

d.

e.

7 My Family

A Listen and match. 🎧 TR: 7.1

1.

2.

3.

a.

b.

c.

B Point and say.

A **Listen and number.** TR: 7.2

B **Draw three of your toys.** Then say. TR: 7.3

This is my train.

A **Listen and number.** TR: 7.4

B **Draw your family.** Then match and say. TR: 7.5

This is my mum. She's happy.

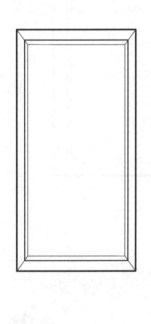
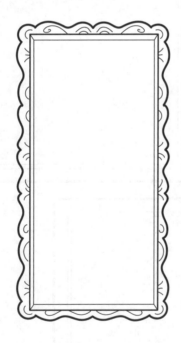

A Trace and write.

Ss
sun

Tt
tea

Uu
umbrella

Vv
van

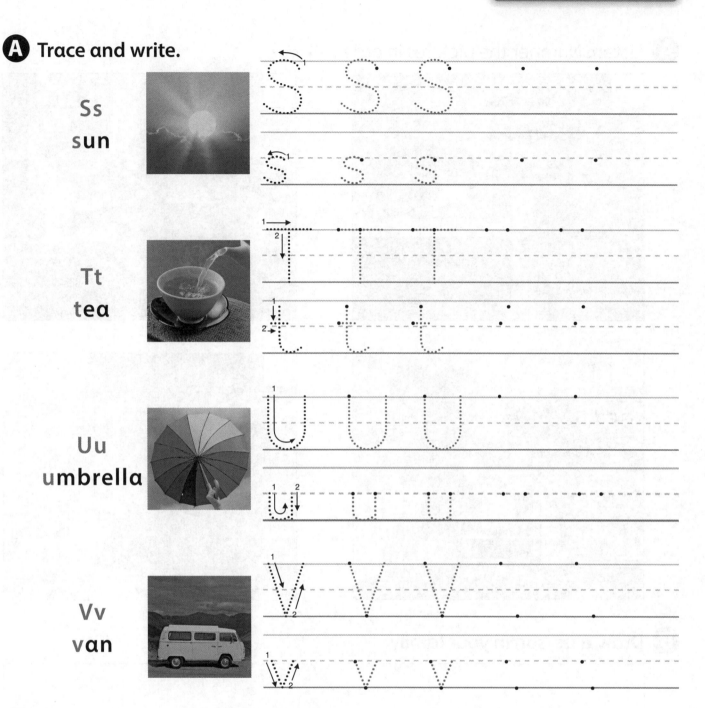

B Listen. Write the first letter. 🎧 TR: 7.6

1. t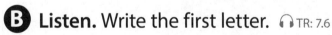

2.

3.

4.

A **Listen.** Number the pictures in order. 🎧 TR: 7.7

B Draw a person in your family.

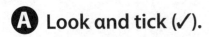

VALUE
Help others.

A Look and tick (✓).

1.

2.

3.

B Draw.

Help others.

8 My Body

A **Listen and number.** 🎧 TR: 8.1

head ☐

eye ☐

nose ☐

arm ☐

☐ ear

☐ mouth

☐ hand

☐ leg

B **Trace and say.** Then colour.

54

A Listen and number. 🎧 TR: 8.2

B Draw and say. 🎧 TR: 8.3

I've got two eyes.

A **Listen and colour.** 🎧 TR: 8.4

1.

2.

B **Draw and colour a silly creature.** Then say.

I've got <u>five</u> <u>arms</u>!

A Trace and write.

Ww
water

Xx
box

Yy
yo-yo

Zz
zebra

B Listen. Write the letter you hear: *w*, *x*, *y* or *z*. 🎧 TR: 8.5

1. _____

2. _____

3. _____

4. _____

A **Listen.** Number the pictures in order. 🎧 TR: 8.6

B Draw a mask.

VALUE

Be kind.

A Look and tick (✓).

1.

2.

3.

B Draw.

Be kind.

A **Listen.** Write a tick (✓) or a cross (✗). 🎧 TR: 8.7

1.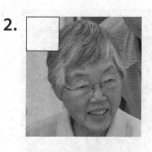
2.
3.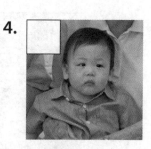
4.

5.
6.
7.

B **Circle the odd one out.** Then say.

1.

2.

3.

C **Happy or sad?** Draw and say. 🎧 TR: 8.8

This is my mum.
She's happy!

D **Colour and say.** 🎧 TR: 8.9

 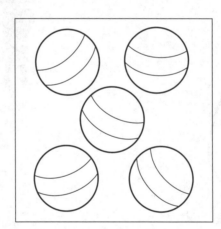 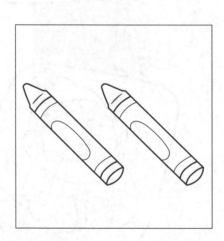

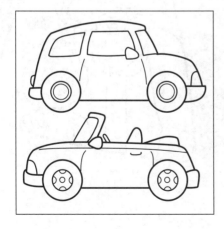 

I've got two cats.
They're brown.

Colour. Point and say.

FINISH

MILK

Word List

Unit 1
apple
bag
cake
Goodbye.
Hello.
Sing.
Sit down.
Stand up.
Thank you.

Unit 2
book
chair
crayon
desk
duck
egg
fish
pencil
teacher
1 one
2 two
3 three
4 four
5 five
6 six

Unit 3
ball
black
blue
brown
car
doll
goat
green
hippo
igloo
orange
red
robot
teddy
train
white
yellow

Unit 4
big
bird
cat
cow
dog
horse
jam
king
lizard
rabbit
small
7 seven
8 eight
9 nine
10 ten
11 eleven
12 twelve

Unit 5
bread
chicken
fruit
juice
milk
monkey
nuts
ostrich
rice
water

Unit 6
cold
happy
hot
hungry
pencil
pink
quilt
rain
sad
thirsty

Unit 7
baby
brother
dad
grandma
grandpa
mum
sister
sun
tea
umbrella
van

Unit 8
arm
box
ear
eye
hand
head
leg
mouth
nose
water
yo-yo
zebra